TREVOR ROWLEY and JOHN WOOD

DESERTED
VILLAGES

SHIRE ARCHAEOLOGY

2

Cover illustration
Aerial view of an earthwork deserted village site one mile
south-west of Aston Abbotts, Buckinghamshire (grid reference SP 842188).

Published by
SHIRE PUBLICATIONS LTD
Cromwell House, Church Street, Princes Risborough,
Aylesbury, Bucks, HP17 9AJ, UK.

Series Editor: James Dyer

ISBN 0 85263 593 1

First published 1982, reprinted 1985

Set by Avocet, Aylesbury, and printed in Great Britain by
C. I. Thomas & Sons (Haverfordwest) Ltd,
Press Buildings, Merlins Bridge, Haverfordwest.

Acknowledgements

We have drawn generously on the published works of the great
pioneers of the investigation of deserted villages, Professor M. W.
Beresford, Mr J. G. Hurst and Professor W. G. Hoskins, and we
gratefully acknowledge our debt to them. We would particularly like
to thank Shirley Hermon for preparing the typescript and Hilary
Welch for drawing the final plans.

We are most grateful to the following for permission to reproduce
or redraw their plans: fig. 1, map revision, from MVRG lists by
Robin Glassock with assistance from Alan Nash, cartography by
Michael Young and Pamela Lucas, Department of Geography,
Cambridge University; fig. 3, James Bond; fig. 4, John Steane and
James Bond; fig. 17, Phil Page; and the Cambridge Committee
for Aerial Photography for permission to reproduce plates 1, 2,
3, 5, 6, 9, 10, 12, 13, 15, 16, 19; plate 17, Mr R. B. B. Gibbs for
photographing the Boarstall map in the Buckinghamshire Record
Office; plate 18, All Souls College, Oxford.

Thanks are also due to Linda Rowley for preparing the index.

Contents

Preface

Although the study of deserted villages is relatively young, some three thousand have been identified in England alone over the past thirty years. Many of these have been found by amateurs working as individuals or in groups. It is the aim of this publication to draw attention to this fascinating aspect of the English landscape and to encourage others to visit known sites and discover new ones.

It is our hope too that some readers will be tempted into recording village sites: only a small proportion of known sites have been surveyed even in the most cursory way. The task of making a recording may sound rather daunting, but after a few days experience it becomes a fairly simple and extremely rewarding exercise. However you approach the topic, we hope that deserted villages bring as much pleasure to you as they have to us.

Trevor Rowley, John Wood
Oxford

List of illustrations

1
What is a deserted village?

Do deserted villages exist?

'He had heard divers ancient people say and affirm that in old time there was a town within the parish of Middleton called Kiplingcotes. That he hath often seen the plain marks and indication of divers frontsteads and the foundations of divers houses, and also a large hole where there was a well for the use of the inhabitants of Kiplingcotes. There was a chapel, and the lesser of the two bells in Middleton Church was brought thither when the town was demolished.'

Such was the evidence of William Wilkinson, yeoman, in a dispute over tithes in 1689 (Beresford, 1954). The plaintiff was concerned to prove that there had never been a village or church at Kiplingcotes and that no tithes had ever been paid. Another witness to the Kiplingcotes enquiry refused 'to believe that there was ever any such town'. Nevertheless such a village did once exist and had been deserted along with many other settlements during the later middle ages.

It is now estimated that hidden in the English countryside there are at least three thousand abandoned villages (fig. 1). Yet many people have been sceptical about the very existence of deserted villages. As recently as 1946 the great economic historian Sir John Clapham remarked: 'Deserted villages are singularly rare in England.' Nevertheless, some had already been identified by local historians in the eighteenth and nineteenth centuries. As early as 1846 the Reverend J. Wilson undertook excavations at the deserted village of Woodperry not far from Oxford. In Oliver Goldsmith's *The Deserted Village* (1770), the preface was addressed to the sceptics, whose number included Dr Johnson: 'I have taken all possible pains in my country excursions for these four or five years past to be certain of what I allege. Some of my friends think that the depopulation of villages does not exist, but I am myself satisfied.'

It seems that the poem was based on actual experience rather than romantic fantasy. Goldsmith visited Nuneham Courtenay in Oxfordshire at the time that the first Lord Harcourt was levelling the old village and replacing it with a new model village on the line of the present Oxford to Henley road, where it can still be seen today. Nuneham was one of very many villages to be moved at about that time in order to create or expand landscaped parks.

Rural settlement patterns have been systematically investigated only since the 1950s. Tribute must be paid to the pioneers of deserted village research: Professor M. W. Beresford, whose *Lost Villages of England* appeared in 1954; and Professor W. G. Hoskins, who published *The Making of the English Landscape* the following year. Such scholars laid the solid foundations for subsequent investigation into abandoned rural settlement. The Deserted Medieval Village Research Group, founded in 1952, under the watchful stewardship of its Secretary for over twenty years, Mr J. G. Hurst, has helped to stimulate and co-ordinate further investigation. The change of name to the Medieval Village Research Group reflects a developing awareness by geographers, historians and archaeologists that deserted villages must be seen in the context of the continuously evolving landscape. (Further information about the group can be obtained from Mrs B. Ewins, The Secretary, Medieval Village Research Group, 51 The Avenue, Kew Gardens, Richmond, Surrey, TW9 2AL.)

Deserted villages in the landscape

The term *village* is not an easy one to define. Because of the enormous variety of settlement in the countryside we need to employ a broad definition of *village*, which will enable us to consider hamlets and clusters of farms on the one hand and small towns on the other. In parts of East Anglia and the South-west settlement has traditionally been scattered, while in the Midlands communities have tended to be more compact. For our purpose the *village* will consist of a group of families living in a collection of houses and having a sense of community, irrespective of its actual size.

Settlement history is much more fluid than we might imagine by examining the countryside today. The tranquillity of many villages suggests to the casual observer that they have existed more or less in their present form since they were first established; but the apparent timelessness of many villages is deceptive: prosperous towns can decline, and tiny hamlets grow – settlements are constantly changing. Villages have prospered, declined and migrated to new sites for a wide variety of social, cultural and economic reasons as they have responded to changing conditions.

Ever since man began to live in nucleated rural communities in

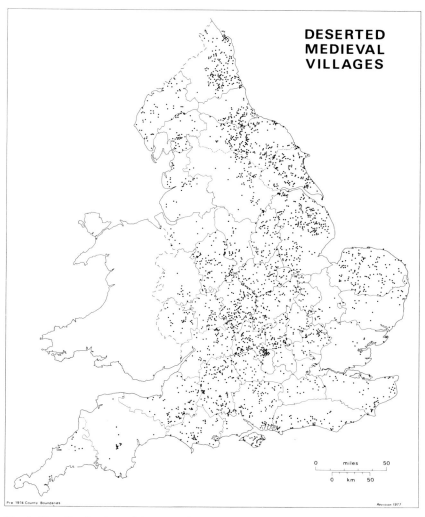

Fig. 1. The distribution of deserted villages (up to 1977). The map is incomplete as sites in some counties, particularly in the West, have yet to be incorporated (*cf* fig. 17).

England there have always been some which have periodically failed completely. There are deserted villages which date from prehistoric times and others which have been abandoned within living memory. Some have been refounded, such as Cublington (Buckinghamshire), which was deserted in 1340 but repopulated again by 1410. Thousands of other villages have diminished in size without ever being completely deserted; these fall into the category of *shrunken* villages.

The (Deserted) Medieval Village Research Group decided in 1952 to distinguish between shrunken and deserted villages according to the number of surviving houses. If there were fewer than three inhabited houses, the village was classified as being deserted: communities with more than three houses were merely shrunken. This is necessarily an artificial distinction: the same dynamic processes of settlement geography have been at work, whether a settlement has been completely or only partially abandoned.

Why study deserted villages?

A visit to the remains of a community which once thrived – a lonely farmhouse, isolated church or bumpy field – is in itself an evocative experience. Deserted villages frequently occupy attractive rural sites, making them intrinsically pleasant to study. We imagine the busy life of the village in its heyday and perhaps see, as Bishop Latimer recognised in his sermon to King Edward VI in 1549, that 'where there have been a great many householders and inhabitants there is now but a shepherd and his dog'. In their turn the sheep may have long since disappeared and modern agricultural techniques reduced the village remains to nothing more than different coloured markings in the growing corn (cropmarks) (see plate 3). Other villages may be truly 'lost' and no trace of them visible on the surface at all. Apart from the aesthetic pleasures of studying deserted villages, they provide important evidence for various disciplines at a variety of levels.

To the economic historian, historical geographer and archaeologist, deserted villages have immense value as reservoirs of information: they provide a window into history, uncluttered by later buildings and developments, and enable us to view a settlement as it was at the time it was deserted. Deserted villages preserve contemporary patterns of occupation, topography and buildings. They also help us interpret the population size and structure of former settlements as well as revealing much about their economy and everyday life. In some cases we are able to discover the reason why they were abandoned. They also help the historical geographer

Plate 1. The borough of Caus, Shropshire, a failed medieval town – the wooded area covers a massive Norman castle. The town declined along with its strategic function in the late middle ages. There is now a single farm here.

to reconstruct former patterns of settlement and land use and thus provide a barometer for economic historians to measure more general economic and social changes in England, reflecting, for example, the development of the late medieval textile industry. Deserted villages are repositories of historical information, telling us about the nature of the world in which they existed and about the landscape around us today.

The sites of deserted villages are still being found, but they are also disappearing at an alarming rate, largely as a result of modern farming techniques as the landscape adapts to changing economic pressures. For instance, a recent analysis of deserted villages in Herefordshire recorded on aerial photographs taken in the 1960s showed that 75 per cent of them had earthworks which had been damaged or completely removed by 1980. There is therefore a pressing need to locate and record these sites before the vast majority are destroyed without trace.

2
When and why were villages deserted?

'There was probably never a decade in the middle ages which did not see the death of one or more English village. A village was as mortal as a man.' (Beresford, 1954)

Beyond Domesday: Anglo-Saxon and Norman village desertions

The first accurate national census in Britain was not taken until 1801; it is therefore possible only to estimate the total population before this. Nevertheless, documentary sources and the archaeological record do enable us to identify general demographic trends. A population decline in the late Roman and post-Roman period appears to have been followed by steady growth from mid Anglo-Saxon times (c 700) until about 1300.

Despite this growth, over one hundred abandoned settlements have been located from the Anglo-Saxon period. For example, the village of West Stow (Suffolk) was quite suddenly, though peacefully, deserted in the mid seventh century after being occupied for about 250 years. Many villages underwent major change of plan or site, leaving evidence of their migration and mutation. North Elmham (Norfolk), for example, was completely redesigned several times before its final desertion in the early twelfth century. Excavations at Maxey (Cambridgeshire), Sutton Courtenay (Oxfordshire) and St Neots (Cambridgeshire) have also demonstrated a continual change of layout. The reasons for such alterations are not yet fully understood. Such early desertions rarely appear in the fragmentary surviving documentary records but they can be studied by archaeologists, who often locate these sites by accident, frequently as a result of redevelopment, such as road construction.

The first major surviving document is the Domesday Book; in this great survey of William the Conqueror's new kingdom, conducted in 1086, we are able to obtain some hints and references to the process of settlement abandonment in the eleventh century. For example, over a third of the vills of Yorkshire and almost all those of

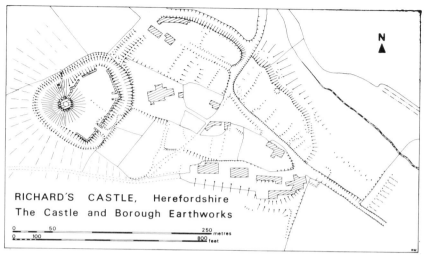

RICHARD'S CASTLE, Herefordshire
The Castle and Borough Earthworks

Fig. 2. Richard's Castle, Herefordshire. The earthworks of the deserted medieval borough: traces of the regular burgage plots can be seen in the large town bailey.

Lancashire were listed as wholly or partially waste. Years of raids by Scandinavian armies and pirates must have taken a heavy toll, but much destruction seems to have been the result of William's terrible 'harrying of the North' between 1069 and 1070. Nevertheless, most of these places were eventually repopulated.

Permanent desertions because of war or pillage were relatively rare in England – sheer pressure of population meant that villages which were violently destroyed were normally soon re-established. The Domesday Book demonstrates that there were some permanent desertions: several villages were cleared to make way for the King's hunting areas in the New Forest (Hampshire), while other Norman lords destroyed Saxon houses to build their castles. At Norwich, for instance, 113 houses were destroyed. Excavation at Oxford and at several other centres has revealed Saxon houses sealed beneath castle earthworks: at Eaton Socon (Cambridgeshire) excavations have shown that the twelfth-century castle overlay the whole village including the church.

In other circumstances the building of a castle often encouraged settlement growth. There are many instances in the Welsh borderland of small towns and villages created within the shadow of

Marcher lords' castles (plate 1). These castles and their associated settlements tended to decline when the border troubles subsided, making the castles' protection and the strategic siting of the settlement unnecessary (fig. 2).

Expansion 1100-1300

During the twelfth century there were important developments in the landscape. Population pressure was the most important and resulted in the creation of many new towns and villages and the expansion of existing settlements throughout England. At the same time, the foundation of the great Cistercian abbeys and other religious houses reflected the emergence of the church as a powerful economic and political force.

During this period (*c* 1100–1250) wasteland and the surviving woodland were being cleared: contemporary documents continuously record *assarts* or clearings in waste and wood. In an attempt to feed the growing numbers of people the limits of cultivation were pushed as far as possible into marginal land. This process has been dramatically demonstrated by aerial photographs, which have located traces of medieval farming high above the present level of cultivation, for example in the Pennines and on Dartmoor (plate 2).

Growth continued until the mid thirteenth century and is reflected in large numbers of new boroughs, established by the Crown, civil lords and church authorities. In Staffordshire, for example, only three boroughs were recorded in 1086 but by 1399 there were twenty-two. In Devon, the number rose from five in 1086 to eighteen by 1238. This pattern is repeated in Suffolk and throughout the rest of England. These new creations experienced a variable rate of success. For instance, about half of Devon's boroughs, most of which were founded during this period, failed to survive in the long term. Some of these new boroughs were based on existing villages such as Cestersover (Warwickshire) (plate 3, fig. 3), which was granted market rights in 1257 but subsequently abandoned; a series of plots can still be seen in the form of earthworks laid out at right angles to the main village street.

Monasteries were engaged in draining fens and reclaiming heaths and moorland, partly because they had the resources to do so, and also because much of land granted to them was of marginal quality. The Cistercian rule insisted on solitude for the monks, and in the increasingly crowded twelfth century villages sometimes had to be removed to enable abbeys to be founded. As the contemporary critic Walter Map wrote: 'you could say "grass grows green where Troy

Plate 2. Hound Tor, Devon. The outlines of the stone-based longhouses can be seen in the centre of the aerial photograph. Traces of former field systems can be seen in the surrounding area.

Plate 3. Cestersover, Warwickshire. The ploughed-out remains of the deserted settlement can be seen in the form of cropmarks (*cf* fig. 3).

town stood". They create a solitude that may be solitaries' (Allison, 1970). The monks' Ledge-book for Stoneleigh Abbey records that they: 'settled in the place where Coulefield Grange now is, having moved away those who lived there to the village now called Hurste' (Beresford, 1954).

Revesby Abbey (Northamptonshire) was given all the land in the three villages of Revesby, Thoresby and Stichesby by the Earl of Lincoln on its foundation in 1142. The Earl's charter confirms that seven peasants have taken land in exchange and thirty-one accepted their freedom – possibly by moving to a nearby town. When Byland Abbey (North Yorkshire) was founded close to Rievaulx, the villagers were moved to a new site some distance away – confusingly, now called Old Byland. The original village probably stood just south of what is now Tile House Farm, but the monks soon discovered that their bells were too close to those of Rievaulx Abbey. Byland Abbey itself was moved to its present position 4 miles (6.4 km) away, and in time New Byland village grew up beside the new buildings.

Setback and decline
About 1250-1300, when the population had reached a peak of between three and five million, it began to decline. Various explanations have been offered for this reverse, the most plausible being that the population had simply passed the limit to which it could grow, given the economy, technology and agriculture of the time. Disease and soil exhaustion then became factors in reducing population. The tax assessments known as the Inquisitions of the Ninth, of 1341-2, recorded soil infertility and bad weather as reasons why the taxation liability of villages should be reduced. At Cuxham (Oxfordshire) wheat which had yielded a splendid 8.3 to every one quarter sown in 1288-99 was only yielding half as much fifty years later. Harvests failed in 1315, 1316 and 1321, and terrible sheep and cattle murrains occurred in 1313-17 and 1319-21 respectively. Storms on the coasts removed thousands of acres of agricultural land in Cambridgeshire, Kent and Sussex; while in the North the Scots periodically raided deep into Yorkshire, destroying perhaps 140 villages in 1218 alone. Some of these settlements, such as Mortham (North Yorkshire), were burnt in 1346 and were never rebuilt. None of these factors can fully explain the fall in population by themselves; but certainly decline had already set in when at the end of June 1348 a ship docked at Melcombe Regis (Dorset) bringing with it the Black Death.

Traditionally the Black Death has been blamed for dramatically

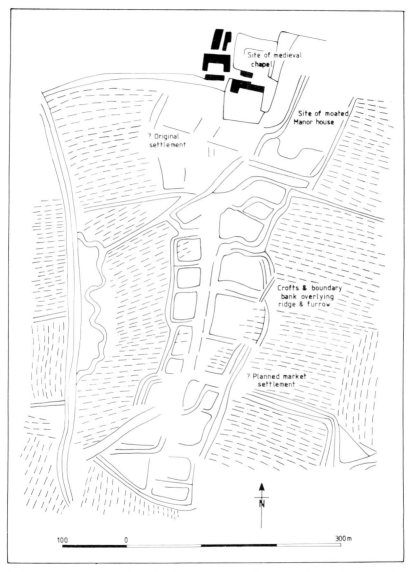

Site of medieval chapel

Site of moated Manor house

? Original settlement

Crofts & boundary bank overlying ridge & furrow

? Planned market settlement

N

100   0   300 m

Fig. 3. Cestersover, Warwickshire. Diagrammatic plan of the deserted village taken from an aerial photograph, showing the extension of the village over areas of former arable.

reducing the population in the years 1349-51, but few villages were totally and permanently deserted for that reason alone. Good farming land soon attracted fresh settlers as at Clothall (Hertfordshire). However we should not underestimate its impact. Standelf, Tusmore and Tilgarsley in Oxfordshire were totally wiped out and the records of the institutions of clergy for 1348-9 tell a grim story: at Winterbourne Clenston (Dorset) four successive rectors were appointed to the living and many other villages received two or more new parish priests over a period of a year or so. The plague served to accelerate decline and the overall long-term effect was devastating, especially as the disease then became endemic for centuries.

At this time too a number of the boroughs founded with such enthusiasm before 1250 began to fail, as did several of the poorer and smaller villages which had been established on unpromising land under population pressure during the twelfth century. Thrislington (County Durham), for example, declined over a long period until one farm was able to take over all the land. As tenancies became vacant and labour scarcer, peasants were able to take advantage of the situation: they moved from marginal lands to better soils, amalgamated holdings and took long leases on favourable terms. Villages whose lands were poorest or where the terms on which land was held were unattractive shrank in size. Fordington (Lincolnshire), for example, had so few parishioners by 1450 that the parish was amalgamated with neighbouring Unceby. At the bleak marginal site of Cold Weston in south Shropshire the settlement was in a decline before the Black Death; in 1341 the parish was assessed at 4s 8d compared with £5 3s in 1291. The assessors stated that there 'had once been abundance of cattle here', but that they had decreased in number because of the murrain which had hit the region. The account continues: 'the chapel is in a waste place and the living had been presented to four parsons within the year but none of them would stay, and there are only two tenants living by great labour and want, and others have absconded.'

Monasteries and colleges are among those landlords who found it increasingly hard to attract tenants. At Ibstone, on the Chilterns, a windmill constructed at some expense by Merton College, Oxford, in the 1290s lay derelict by 1330 through a lack of tenant farmers who needed to grind their corn there. At Upton (Gloucestershire) the Bishop of Worcester was unable to find tenants for his arable land, so he turned it over to sheep grazing (see plate 11); and at Wollashill (Worcestershire) a similar process occurred. As Professor Beresford remarks: 'The natural residual crop on land which

Plate 4. Fawsley, Northamptonshire. The church stands isolated in the grounds of Fawsley House, built by the Knightley family, who were responsible for depopulating the village for sheep pasture in the fifteenth century.

had been abandoned was grass, so long as you had enough animals to keep the scrub from encroaching' (Beresford, 1954).

Pastures and profits

'Till now I thought the proverb did but jest which said a black sheep was a biting beast' (Thomas Bastard, *Epigrams, c* 1600).

As the wool industry developed it became more profitable. In west and south-west England pasture had always been important, while in Kent and Essex there had long been a mixed economy. In the Midland counties of Oxfordshire, Northamptonshire and Leicestershire, however, much good arable land was now converted to excellent pasture. Landlords began to build up their flocks in a more determined fashion and it became worthwhile to remove villages, particularly those already in decline. Sheep rearing required much less labour than arable husbandry, and after desertion even the village sites themselves could be used for grazing (plate 4).

Most deserted village sites in England date from the period of the greatest prosperity of the wool trade in the fifteenth century, though depopulation for pasture continued well into the late Tudor period. The peak of desertion came at different times in different parts of the country, with the Midlands generally much earlier than the North. As the fifteenth century progressed the government began to take an interest in events. There were constant complaints from evicted tenants, and the evidence of ruined villages all over England was there for all to see. The depopulating landlords became a scapegoat for social and economic problems and were a popular target for contemporary pamphleteers and even dramatists:

'I can compare our rich misers to nothing so fitly as
a whale. A'plays and tumbles, driving the poor fry
before him, and at least devours them all at a mouthful;
such whales have I heard on i' the land, who never leave
gaping till they've swallowed the whole parish, church,
steeple, bells and all.' (*Pericles, Prince of Tyre*, Act 2)

Yet all sections of society, even prosperous peasants, were turning to sheep farming, and, of course, more villages survived than were totally depopulated. Nevertheless, while a statute of 1402 declared that the monks and other subjects of the king should not be insulted by being called '*depopulatores agrum*' (depopulators of the fields), an Act of 1489 made it an offence to convert open fields to pasture if it involved the removal of smallholdings over 20 acres (8.1 ha). Overlords were expected to take action to ensure that, in proven cases, arable holdings were reinstated. The preamble to the 1489 Act describes why the government was concerned:

'Great inconveniences daily doth increase by desolation
and pulling down and wilfull waste of houses and Towns
within that his (i.e. the king's) realm, and laying to
pasture lands which customarily have been used in tillage,
whereby idleness – ground and beginning of all mischiefs
– daily doth increase, for where in some Towns two hundred
persons were occupied and lived by their lawful labours,
now be there occupied 2 or 3 herdmen and the residue fallen
in idleness; the husbandry, which is one of the greatest
commodities of the realm, is greatly decayed; churches destroyed; the service of God withdrawn; the bodies there
buried not prayed for; the patron and curate wronged; the
defence of this land against our enemies outwards feebled
and impaired: to the great displeasure of God, to the
subversion of the policy and good rule of this land.'

This polemic probably overstates the case but it is no accident that, during the sixteenth century, the landless peasant or vagrant is a common character in political tracts. The same century also saw the development of 'squatting' by landless peasants on the edges of common waste on a large scale. Contemporary writers make it clear that this was a classic conflict between private profit and social welfare – the interests of the overlords coincided with those of the depopulator and the grazier.

Nothing was done until a new Act against village depopulation was passed in 1515, followed in 1517 and 1518 by Cardinal Wolsey's Commissions of Inquiry to enforce the legislation. Although we cannot take all the evidence literally, these enquiries provide us with interesting insights into the depopulating process. For instance, it was reported that the Prior of Bicester had held five houses with 30 acres (12.1 ha) attached to each and 200 acres (80.9 ha) of his own at Wretchwick (Oxfordshire).

> 'He held this land on the second of March 1489 when those messuages were laid waste and thrown down, and lands formerly used for arable he turned over to pasture for animals, so three ploughs are now out of use there, and eighteen people who used to work on that land and earn their living there and who dwelled in the houses have gone away to take to the roads in their misery, and to seek their bread elsewhere and so are led into idleness.'

Not all those who dwelled in the houses can have been as poor as this statement would suggest. Wretchwick rentals for 1432-7 give the tenants' names, their holdings, and those holdings which were vacant. About a dozen families lived there, several of whom farmed extra holdings for which the priory could not find tenants, and some of these families, at least, are likely to have accumulated enough movable capital and expertise to start again elsewhere. The site can be clearly seen today as earthworks and banks surrounding the aptly named Middle Wretchwick Farm (fig. 4).

Privacy and pride: the creation of parks

It has been estimated that, by 1500, there were three times as many sheep as humans in England. However from the mid fifteenth century the population had once more begun to increase. The profit motive still dominated the removal of villages but, already, this was being augmented by social factors as the status-conscious began to

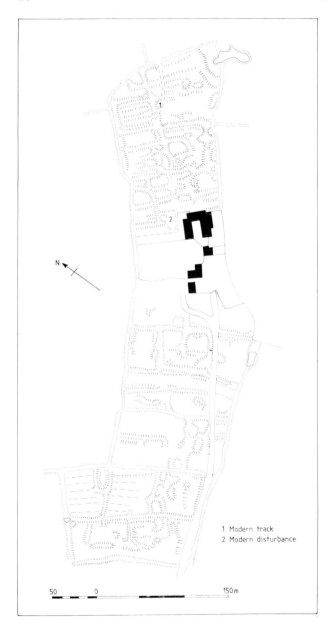

1 Modern track
2 Modern disturbance

50   0   150m

Fig. 4.
Wretchwick,
Oxfordshire. A
surveyed plan of
the extensive
earthworks of a
typical Midland
deserted medieval
village.

Plate 5. Berrington Park, Herefordshire. Traces of the fields of the former settlement can be seen within the great park of Berrington House.

build exclusive parks for themselves, often incorporating landscaped gardens. As early as 1421 Henry V's brother, the Duke of Bedford, removed Fulbrook (Warwickshire), to make way for a park while in 1440 a licence was granted to empark 200 acres (80.9 ha) at Pendley (Hertfordshire), where a sizable village was removed. Such early parks had aesthetic and social overtones quite apart from the economic importance of their timber, grazing and game. Their development mirrors that of the country houses with which they were associated, and over the next three centuries park and house became larger and increasingly concerned with aesthetics and extravagance (plate 5). Emparking reached its zenith in the eighteenth century, when the removal of villages to create or enlarge parks was a widespread phenomenon. Ickworth (Suffolk), Pudding Norton (Norfolk), Wimpole (Cambridgeshire) and other examples supplement Goldsmith's Auburn, identified above with Nuneham Courtenay (Oxfordshire), where

'The man of wealth and pride
Takes up a space that many poor supplied;
Space for his lake, his park's extended bounds
Space for his horses, equipage and hounds.'
                              (The Deserted Village, 1770.)

In other places, the removal of villages and the creation of country houses, parks and gardens occurred together. In the celebrated case of Milton Abbas (Dorset) an entire market town was removed over a period of fifteen years by the first Baron Milton in order to construct his park. In 1673 there had been one hundred houses there, which he replaced with the small, regularly planned estate village. Such model or estate villages were designed to lie out of sight of the great houses and are usually recognisable by their neatly ordered, often identically designed houses, foreshadowing modern housing developments.

The process is well illustrated at Middleton Stoney (Oxfordshire), where a normal open-field village had been enclosed by agreement between the freehold farmers in 1698. During the following century and a quarter the Earls of Jersey, using a small medieval deer park as a base, gradually bought out the freeholders and extended their park until 1825, when the Oxford to Northampton road was diverted from its old route through the village to its present location on the edge of the park. The old village was destroyed and a new village built along the line of the new road (fig. 5). Other examples of this process can be seen at Wimpole (Cambridgeshire) and at Holkham and Houghton in Norfolk; Horninghold (Leicestershire) is an early twentieth-century example.

The creators of parks did not always trouble to rehouse displaced villagers; Stowe and Wootton Underwood (Buckinghamshire), for instance, disappeared altogether. At Hinderskelfe (North Yorkshire), where the Earl of Carlisle constructed Castle Howard, even the church vanished beneath the formal gardens and was not replaced. This practice was criticised by the landscape architect Humphrey Repton:

'I have, on several occasions, ventured to condemn as
false taste that fatal rage for destroying villages or
depopulating a country, under the idea of its being
necessary to the importance of a mansion ... As a
number of labourers constitutes one of the requisites
of grandeur, comfortable habitations for its poor de-
pendants ought to be provided' (Beresford and Hurst, 1971).

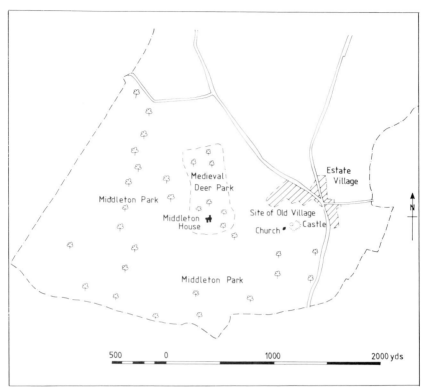

Fig. 5. Middleton Stoney, Oxfordshire. Plan showing how the park was extended from its original small medieval nucleus to its present size and displaced the village in the process.

The building of new country houses did not necessarily mean the removal of a village, however. In some instances the village had already gone, providing an attractive vacant space for a house and park. A good example of this can be seen at Compton Wynyates (Warwickshire), where one of the earliest surviving country houses was built in about 1520 next to the isolated church of the already deserted village. The same process can be seen at Compton Verney (Warwickshire), where the village was abandoned several hundred years before the house was built.

Other reasons for desertion

There are many examples of settlements which were destroyed by

Plate 6. Newbold Grounds, Northamptonshire. Earthworks of a 'classic' deserted medieval village. The house platforms, sunken ways and precinct boundary can be clearly seen. The village is surrounded by ridge and furrow and seems in part, at least, to overlie former ridges.

natural agents and not rebuilt. Fire accidentally but permanently destroyed Bywell on Tyne in 1285, and the sea has removed villages from many parts of the coastline. At Hallsands (Devon) the sea was helped by the deliberate removal and sale of a protective shingle bank at the end of the nineteenth century. Now only a few ruins remain, perched on the cliffs.

Today villages in many parts of Britain are losing their populations at an alarming rate. More than a dozen have been totally deserted since the 1950s. Settlements established close to the mines and mills of the industrial revolution have declined with the industries they served. Until recently the removal of redundant pit

Plate 7. Newbold Grounds after ploughing. The site has been reduced to an irregular pattern of cropmarks which reflect the most deeply engraved features of the former site.

villages in County Durham was encouraged by Durham County Council, who demolished Leasingthorne, for instance, in 1969. Virtually all the seventy pits open in the county in the 1940s are likely to have closed by 1990, and so the process of village decline continues.

The mechanisation of agriculture has also depopulated villages: sixty per cent of those people employed in farming in the 1940s have since left the land. Throughout Britain rural settlements have lost on average a third of their inhabitants as a result. Faxton (Northamptonshire) has been completely deserted since 1945. As people leave the rural areas, shops and schools, bus services and post offices are withdrawn, providing further incentives for people to move away.

Many more villages would be lying in ruins today were it not for the retired, the commuters and weekenders who occupy and maintain the houses in them; but newcomers can do little to restore a disappearing way of life. They can even add to the problems of a village by forcing house prices out of the reach of local people and objecting to efforts to create local employment on aesthetic grounds. While the countryside is opened up to the car owner by an improved road network, this can also damage villages in unexpected ways. Eighteen months after the Brough bypass (Cumbria) was opened, employment in the village shops and hotels had dropped from one hundred and five to thirty-eight. The village was not signposted from the new road and potential customers simply drove past.

Not all villages are left to the rich, the housebound and the elderly. Imber (Wiltshire), for example, was taken over by the army in 1943 to provide a training ground for street fighting, and the inhabitants were evicted. Even the name of the village has now disappeared from the small-scale Ordnance Survey maps, although former villagers are allowed to visit the parish church, encased in a barbed wire enclosure, once a year.

Paradoxically in the twentieth century many villages have disappeared not by the process of abandonment, but through expansion. Villages lying around the edge of large cities have been sucked into the spreading urban areas, while others lying further away have been drastically expanded as dormitory suburbs, so losing much of their original sense of community. Thus the process of rural settlement change continues at an increasing pace into the late twentieth century; but despite many vicissitudes the village remains an extraordinarily flexible unit of human occupation.

3
What do deserted villages look like?

Village desertion and subsequent land use

Villages which were deserted before 1300 have tended to leave little trace above ground. Early peasant houses were generally built of wood, turf or unbaked earth and do not survive in earthwork form although occasionally a few outlines may be visible as cropmarks. Most of the best preserved Anglo-Saxon village remains have been found beneath castle earthworks which have protected them from later erosion, as at Goltho (Lincolnshire), while the remains of West Stow (Suffolk) were protected by a natural bank of sand which was deposited over the site in medieval times. From the thirteenth century onwards, in parts of England stone-built peasant houses were constructed, leaving more substantial remains after they were abandoned. In the case of villages depopulated in order to build castles or abbeys during the early middle ages the remains will normally have been destroyed or damaged beyond recognition.

Many deserted villages in England were abandoned in the later medieval period, and the sites converted to permanent pasture. Some of these sites have survived as earthworks, although in recent years there has been a substantial ploughing-up campaign which has resulted in the conversion of much former permanent pasture to arable and the consequent destruction of earthwork sites. The process of such destruction by ploughing can be seen in plates 6 and 7. Surviving pasture sites provide the 'classic' form of earthwork deserted medieval villages.

The creation of parkland generally obscured former village or even town remains; much of the original town of Milton Abbas (Dorset), for example, lies beneath an artificial lake. In some cases traces of the former settlement will be visible in the form of lighter marks, commonly called *parch marks*.

Mineral working on a large scale is also responsible for much destruction. At West Whelpington (Northumberland), for instance, a settlement which was finally depopulated about 1720, the whole hill on which the village stood has been gradually quarried away. Similarly the remains of an Anglo-Saxon deserted settlement at Catholme (Staffordshire) have disappeared as a consequence of

Plate 8. The isolated church of St Devereux, Herefordshire. The line of the village main street is today marked by a hollow way.

gravel working. Numerous settlements of all periods have been destroyed since the 1960s on the sand and gravel terraces of the major river systems by a similar process. Urban sprawl has engulfed the sites of many former villages, both extant and deserted. St Pancras station in London, for instance, stands on the site of a former deserted medieval village. Forces of nature, too, contribute to the destructive process. Changes in river courses and coastal erosion eat away at the archaeological remains of earlier settlement sites, leaving little except perhaps legends of bells tolling beneath the water.

Isolated churches

The village church often survived when the village it served was abandoned (plates 8 and 9). This was not necessarily because churches were more solidly built than the surrounding houses, or for fear of divine retribution if they should be demolished, but because they belonged to a large independent organisation with its own rights, records and revenues. The church had a vested interest in the tithes and dues from a parish, as demonstrated during the

Plate 9. Wolfhampcote and Braunstonbury (Warwickshire/Northamptonshire). Two deserted villages divided by a stream which forms the county boundary. The photograph incorporates all the characteristic features of the 'classic' earthwork deserted villages: an isolated church, village earthworks, a moated site, fishponds and ridge and furrow.

Kiplingcotes enquiry (see page 5). Besides, parish churches would continue to serve nearby farms and hamlets long after the village was depopulated.

The now isolated churches of former villages can be seen all over England. East Anglia is particularly rich in such sites: at Egmere (Norfolk), for example, the church was partly demolished in Henry VIII's time; close by there are two further ruined churches at Quarles and Waterden. In Devon, the dramatic impact of the isolated church at Brentor, with its associated earthworks, is strengthened by its occupation of an imposing hilltop position.

Not every isolated church indicates the site of a deserted village, however. In Suffolk, for example, some may have been built as private chantries or chapels for the wealthy. Such was the origin of Gipping church, which was constructed by Sir James Tyrell in 1484-5, and there may be other reasons for a church now standing by itself. However, if you are just beginning to identify deserted villages, the isolated parish church (of antiquity) marked on the 1:50,000 Ordnance Survey maps is as good a starting place as any.

Earthworks

Earthworks in the form of banks and hollows, known affectionately as 'lumps and bumps', are the principal visible evidence for deserted villages. Such earthworks sometimes spread over several modern fields, and the clearest overall impression of what they represent is usually obtained from the air or from a ground plan resulting from a survey (fig. 6).

The roadways leading to the site of an abandoned village are sometimes noticeably sunken below the surrounding fields and often lead into the former streets and roads of the settlement. Erosion by animals and carts over many years combines with weather action to create these *hollow-ways*, which are a common feature of deserted village sites. Often surviving country roads of antiquity have been worn down in a similar manner.

In stony areas raised mounds indicate former house sites, although sometimes the stones from the walls have been deliberately 'robbed' out, tending to create a more complicated pattern of earthworks. In areas where turf, timber and clay were the principal building materials the house areas may not be significantly raised above the general ground level and in some cases actually appear as slight square or rectangular depressions (fig. 7).

The house areas will be surrounded by those of outbuildings and boundaries to yards and paddocks (tofts and crofts). The houses with their closes form the core of the village earthworks and are often surrounded by a boundary bank which divided the inhabited area from the fields. Property boundaries represent one of the most ancient man-made elements in the landscape, although those defining individual gardens and house sites were more likely to change. Boundaries are therefore likely to be much older than the house remains visible on the surface. Excavations at deserted village sites have shown that within the tofts houses could be rebuilt on several different alignments without altering the basic boundary arrangements.

Earthworks of manor houses can sometimes be detected in the village. These are frequently larger house areas and they can be surrounded by a distinctive demesne or precinct boundary cutting them off from the rest of the village. Sometimes, too, they can be moated and the moat ditch will often be the most prominent earthwork feature on the site (fig. 8). Care should be taken to

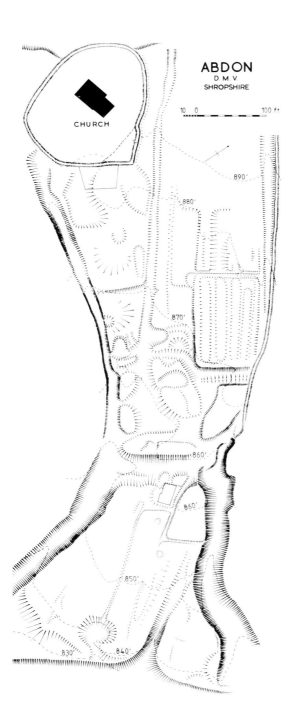

ABDON
D. M. V
SHROPSHIRE

CHURCH

10 0   100 f+

Fig. 6. Abdon. A hachured and contoured plan of a Shropshire deserted village.

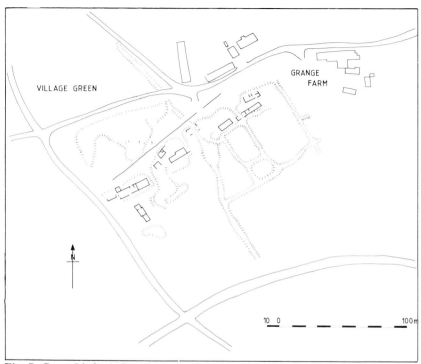

Fig. 7. Great Linford, Buckinghamshire. Plan showing the outline of excavated buildings in relationship to the above-ground earthwork features. (After Mynard.)

determine if the moated site fits comfortably within the general village layout or whether it cuts across earlier features. In the latter case the moated site will represent a manor house or early country house built on the site of the deserted village. Churches and chapels can also be distinguished on some sites. These too tend to be larger rectangular buildings (although not as large as one might imagine) and traces of the churchyard boundary may be identifiable. The alignment of the church earthwork may also be at variance to the general grain of the site. At Old Chalford (Oxfordshire), for instance, a prominent earthwork at the west end of the earthworks of a village is the only one to lie on a strict east to west axis contrary to the local topography, and because of its slightly larger size it has been convincingly interpreted as a chapel (plate 10).

The earthworks of watermills can sometimes be identified in the form of prominent platforms surrounded by channels (normally

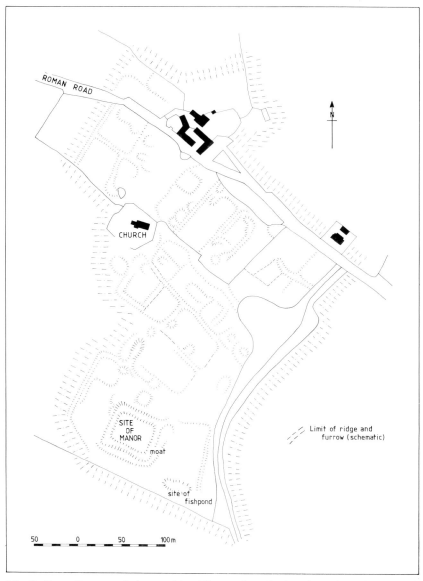

Fig. 8. Great Stretton, Leicestershire. The earthwork plan shows how the moated manor house fits into the general village layout.

Plate 10. Old Chalford, Oxfordshire. This photograph shows the remains of two settlements in the Glyme valley separated by a block of strip lynchets. On the centre left of the picture a rectangular structure lying at variance with the general pattern of earthworks apparently represents a former chapel.

now dry) close to a stream. Most villages possessed at least one watermill during the middle ages, although this often lay at some distance from the main nucleus of the settlement. Other earthworks associated with medieval water management are fish and mill ponds. Often these will be found in close association with the mill site. They normally take the form of a series of large rectangular depressions with earthwork dams, which have usually been breached. In some cases, however, medieval water management earthworks can be extremely complicated, involving the rerouting of long stretches of stream. Windmill mounds are also sometimes found in association with deserted villages.

Fig. 9. Lower Heyford, Oxfordshire. Plan of the strip field system in 1604. The black strips are the parsonage holding and the dotted belong to a single farmer.

Medieval fields

The most common of all earthworks associated with deserted villages, however, are the remains of agricultural activity, normally appearing as *ridge and furrow*. The highly characteristic corrugation is found predominantly in the Midlands but can be located virtually everywhere else in England. A train journey through the Midlands, especially when the winter sun is low in the sky, will reveal, even to the casual observer, substantial areas of ridge and furrow. These earthworks are the remains of former open fields, which in medieval times formed much of the arable land in England. Most villages had several of these large fields, subdivided into narrow strips, which were shared out among the villagers (fig. 9). Bundles of strips made up *furlongs*, which were the basic unit of crop rotation, and often they ran up to the very precinct of the village earthworks.

Under the open-field system each villager was responsible for working his own strips although a collective decision was needed to decide what crops should be grown and where. Each plough team worked up one side of the strip and back down the other, and the effect was always to pile the earth towards the middle, leaving hollows between the plots. If the end of open-field farming coincided

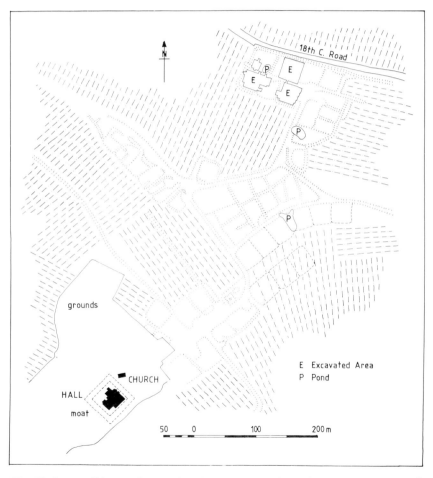

Fig. 10. Barton Blount, Derbyshire. An excavated site which has clear traces of ridge and furrow overlying former house areas (see plate 16). (After G. Beresford.)

with a change of land use to pasture, the form of the strips was preserved. However, the ploughing-up campaign of recent years has taken its toll and the quality of ridge and furrow diminishes annually.

The early enclosures were usually small and irregular in shape, in contrast to those made by Acts of Parliament in the period 1750-1850. The Enclosure Acts took the village fields as a whole and reallocated them in compact parcels of land. Sometimes the new boundaries followed those of the old system; but often they were laid out with no regard to the previous pattern. The centres of many villages declined at this time, as farmers built themselves houses out among the fields of their new holdings.

Care should be taken to see if there are any traces of ridge and furrow underneath enclosures and house areas; this would indicate settlement expansion over former arable (see plate 6 and fig. 10). Conversely in some cases it is quite clear that the settlement has contracted and that ridge and furrow has been laid out over the site of the former community (fig. 10). Earthwork enclosure of former fields is often to be found around the edge of the settlement area; in the North these enclosures often take the shape of long rectangular blocks of land which acted as paddocks behind the garden area of the village. In other parts of England they can be smallish square or rectangular enclosures representing early enclosure of the open-field system. It should be stressed, however, that the visible earthworks only represent the last phase of a village's development before desertion and generally give little indication of the complexity of features which lie beneath (see fig. 7).

4
Archaeology and deserted villages

Deserted villages and the archaeologist

Until relatively recently scholars of medieval history have been largely concerned with great affairs of church and state and the magnificent monuments they produced; but increasingly in recent years attention has been paid to the social and economic structure of society. One of the main areas of recent analysis has been the deserted village. The six hundredth anniversary of the Black Death in 1949 marked the beginning of an upsurge of interest in deserted villages. In studying the village we are examining a central element of the world that was lost with the industrial revolution – all the more fascinating because of its everyday ordinariness. Villages are able to bring us near to the lives of common people of past ages.

Archaeology has already made a significant contribution to our understanding of deserted villages. Although fewer than thirty excavations on deserted village sites took place between 1884 and 1952, an average of five a year were reported between 1953 and 1964, and this scale of work has been continued since then. Some digs have been carefully planned long-term projects, spread over several years, as at Hound Tor (Devon), Goltho (Lincolnshire) (fig. 11) and Upton (Gloucestershire) (plate 11), while at Wharram Percy (North Yorkshire) excavations have taken place every summer since 1950 (fig. 12). Elsewhere emergency operations have been organised to salvage information within weeks or days as sites have been destroyed, but even hurried rescue projects are capable of producing important results.

It is necessary to examine the physical evidence of past communities in order to understand their layout, the nature of their buildings and how village topography developed and changed over the centuries, while the analysis of documentary records provides evidence of the people who built, lived in and finally abandoned the villages. When historical and archaeological approaches are applied jointly village studies benefit considerably. Combined campaigns of investigation have paid rich dividends at sites such as Wharram Percy.

Fig. 11. Goltho, Lincolnshire. The regular village earthworks which have been partly excavated. Late Saxon houses have been found underneath the manor house site. (After G. Beresford.)

Plate 11. An early phase of the excavations at Upton, Gloucestershire, where the lower courses of a medieval longhouse have been uncovered.

The contribution of archaeology: the living picture

It is not easy to obtain a clear picture of the earliest villages. Despite attempts to classify rural settlements according to their layout, there are almost as many categories of village forms as there are villages. The most common plan is linear, with one or two rows of houses laid out along a central street; crossroad villages provide a variation on this theme (plate 12).

The other principal village form is based on the green. This can be square, oval, rectangular or triangular, but in all cases the intention is the same – to provide a broad open space in the heart of the community. The green had various uses, for instance for fairs and markets, for grazing village animals and to provide a meeting place for villagers (plate 13). Many villages were laid out around greens in the middle ages or later and do not owe their regular plans to Anglo-Saxon settlers as was previously thought. There are many instances where a village plan of apparent antiquity can be dated to the ambitious emparking schemes of an eighteenth or nineteenth century squire.

Villages derived from settlements with urban aspirations often have distinctive plans. A grid pattern of streets belonging to a planned medieval town which failed to prosper is visible at Newton (Isle of Wight). New market towns of the twelfth and thirteenth centuries were often designed with a series of long thin *burgage plots* facing a main street or market place and backing on to a *back lane*

Plate 12. An aerial photograph of the deserted village of Wharram Percy seen under snow, which highlights the village features.

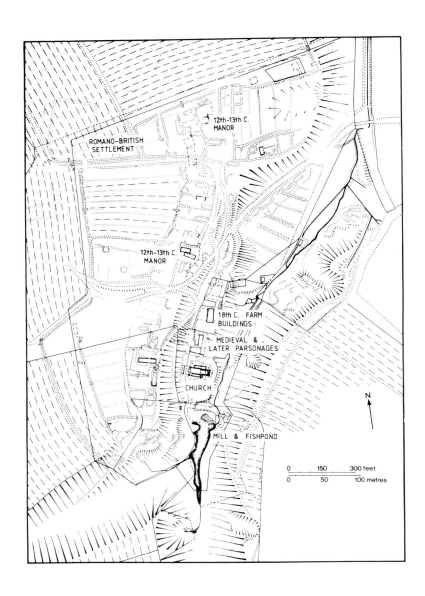

12th-13th C.
MANOR

ROMANO-BRITISH
SETTLEMENT

12th-13th C.
MANOR

18th C. FARM
BUILDINGS

MEDIEVAL &
LATER PARSONAGES

CHURCH

MILL & FISHPOND

N

| 0 | 150 | 300 feet |
| 0 | 50 | 100 metres |

Plate 13. Walworth, County Durham. The earthworks of a deserted green village. House platforms and enclosures can be clearly seen lying around a square green now occupied by a farm and outbuildings. A country house and its gardens occupy the left-hand side of the old village.

Fig. 12 (opposite). Wharram Percy, North Yorkshire. Excavations have been carried out on this extensive earthwork site every year since 1950. The work has shown that the medieval village must now be seen in a much broader chronological perspective, with some boundaries originating in pre-Roman times. (After M. Beresford and J. G. Hurst.)

(this allowed the maximum number of tenants to be accommodated with a frontage well placed for the establishment of shops). Such features can still be seen in the arrangements of many surviving towns and villages which failed to develop beyond their original nuclei.

One of the most striking features of medieval rural settlement is the amount of change that took place within an apparently rigid framework. Churches, manor houses, individual farmsteads and even whole villages were replanned and resited. An early village at

Bardolfeston (Dorset) consisted of a series of rectangular crofts which probably contained timber buildings; but this was overlaid by a later arrangement comprising a single street with two rows of stone houses, on a totally different alignment. A similar realignment took place in the thirteenth century at the deserted village of Seacourt, just outside Oxford.

Village houses

Since the mid 1950s archaeological investigation has enabled the identification of various categories of house plans from the middle ages (fig. 13). At the simplest level there are one-roomed *cots*. They were heated by an open hearth, from which smoke escaped through a louvred or hipped roof. Another basic form was the cellared or sunken-featured building often called by its German name, *Grubenhaus*, which continued in use from the Anglo-Saxon period. Longhouses or laithe-houses can be found in all parts of

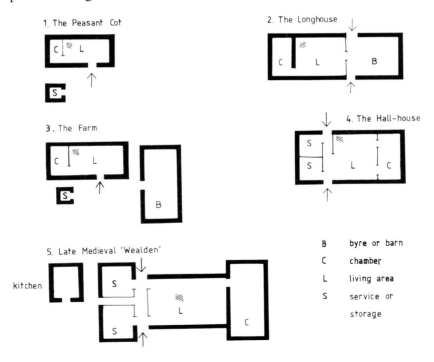

Fig. 13. Medieval house types.

Plate 14. A longhouse still in occupation in Brittany. Animals live in the left-hand part of the building, while humans occupy the right-hand side.

England from the thirteenth and fourteenth centuries (plate 14), although earlier examples have been found at Hound Tor (Devon) (see plate 2). These were divided into two halves by a cross passage between opposing doorways (fig. 14). One end was used as living accommodation for the family, while the other served either as a byre for animals or a store for farm products and equipment. Hall houses of the medieval period were longhouses built by yeoman farmers imitating the house styles of the more wealthy. These had a main hall divided from the service and storage areas by a cross passage, while at the other end of the hall would be a series of smaller rooms, one of which would serve as a bedroom. All these categories shared a common format consisting of an open living area with a number of attached rooms. Large timber halls and barns were sometimes aisled in the same manner as churches.

The size and complexity of the medieval houses naturally reflected the wealth and status of the owners. Detached kitchens and storehouses were associated with early manor houses; and by the later medieval period courtyard farms (fig. 15) appear in a peasant context. There are a number of examples of longhouses being rebuilt in the form of courtyard farms at this time, such as at Gomeldon (Wiltshire) and Upton (Gloucestershire) (fig. 16).

Medieval houses revealed by excavation vary considerably in their plan, size and complexity. They show that the popular impression of medieval squalor is wrong; often the clay floors of peasant houses have been so thoroughly swept that hollows have been created which then had to be levelled up. Partly because of the insubstantial remains of most peasant houses, archaeological deposits on deserted village sites are normally shallow. This leaves a complex stratigraphy which is often difficult to unravel.

Pottery and other small finds

The excavation of deserted medieval village sites produces a broad range of articles, the most common and durable of which are pottery. The pottery type found in the village will reflect the period when the village was occupied, its prosperity and the range of its trading contacts. Apart from the pottery, iron objects are sometimes found if soil conditions are favourable to their preservation. These include blades, nails, spikes, hinges, buckles and horseshoes, as well as padlocks and keys. Bells for animals and small personal ornaments made of copper or bronze, as well as lead weights, are also found.

Stone was used in medieval villages for mortars and querns; whetstones and spindle whorls have also been recovered. Bone objects recovered from sites include combs (often for weaving) and knife handles. Although glass was expensive and treated with great care in medieval times, occasionally glass from bottles, windows or beads is found. From the thirteenth or fourteenth century onwards bricks and tiles appear.

One significant fact to emerge from archaeological work on deserted villages is the relative absence of medieval coins. Whereas on most Romano-British sites coins tend to be plentiful, very few contemporary coins are found on deserted medieval villages, and this confirms that at a peasant level little cash was used. At Upton (Gloucestershire) for example, apart from a collection of Roman coins, five years of excavation produced only a single medieval farthing. Exchange and barter appear to have provided the main mechanisms of trade. Objects were obviously traded over considerable distances. At Wharram Percy, for example, sherds of pottery from the Netherlands, France and Germany have been found.

Environmental evidence

Traces of materials presumed to be perishable may survive even on sites which were deserted at an early date. Wood – so important

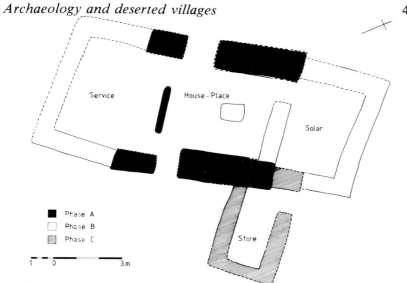

Fig. 14. Abdon, Shropshire. Interpretation of the various phases of development of an excavated medieval longhouse.

Fig. 15. Caldecote, Hertfordshire. The excavated remains of an early farmyard complex. (After G. Beresford.)

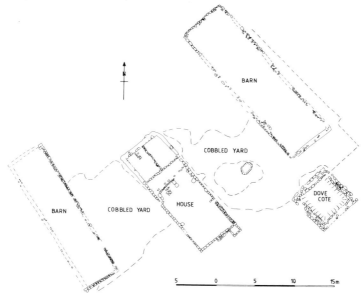

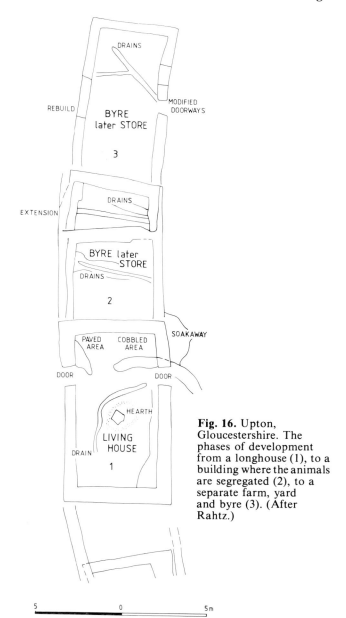

Fig. 16. Upton, Gloucestershire. The phases of development from a longhouse (1), to a building where the animals are segregated (2), to a separate farm, yard and byre (3). (After Rahtz.)

to the pre-industrialised economy – may be preserved either in a waterlogged condition or as charcoal; and seeds can sometimes be recovered which will help to determine which crops were grown. Seeds and other environmental evidence also provide information on the general nature of past landscapes and climatic trends.

Molluscs, beetles and spiders provide information about the environment: some species prefer cool, wet, shady areas, while others prefer open ground. At Wharram Percy the snail shells found indicated open ground in the area of the site, with the presence of hedges and rough vegetation such as 'dank grass, patches of nettles and other tall herbs' (Hurst, 1979).

Animal bones indicate the relative importance of different species to farming in the village and help us understand the breeds which were kept. At Upton (Gloucestershire) cattle apparently provided fifty-three per cent of the meat consumed from domestic stock and were mostly killed before they were three years old, while ninety-seven per cent of the sheep lived beyond two years, suggesting that they were not kept primarily for meat. Pigs provided only three per cent of domestic meat supplies. Medieval animals were much smaller in size than their modern counterparts. Cattle and sheep were apparently slaughtered at about two years, although some of the cattle lived to five years old. Pigs were generally killed at eighteen months. The evidence indicates that many more animals were overwintered than was previously thought, and we should treat the idea of wholesale slaughtering of stock in the autumn with considerable caution. Nevertheless, animals were killed and eaten in considerable quantities; and the methods and techniques of butchery can be studied in the knife-cuts often visible in the bones. At Wharram Percy fish bones were also found, which suggested that fish had been transported in a dried form from the coast.

Human bones can reveal much about population structure, life expectancy and disease. Unbaptised infants were not buried in churchyards, and at Upton a child of three to six months was found buried under the floor of a house. Little work has yet been published on excavated cemeteries from medieval village sites; but it should be possible in time to obtain a reasonably accurate picture of the size and age range of the village population from them, and this will in turn assist the interpretation of documentary records such as tax assessments.

The role of the amateur

Excavation of deserted villages is a complex business, and techniques have been developed by which large areas can be seen in plan and the maximum information retrieved. Untrained and inexperienced digging produces very little of value, and even a small hole or trench dug into a site can cause extensive and irreplaceable damage if not carried out by or under the direction of an archaeologist. The techniques can be learned, but the only satisfactory way to do this is by gaining practical experience on archaeological sites. Some suggestions and addresses for those interested are given in Chapter 8.

Archaeological work is not all excavation, however. In recent years increasing attention has been paid to landscape survey and other non-destructive research, and this by itself produces important results. Even a sketch survey which shows the general layout of earthworks and other topographical features may be the only record made of a site before it is destroyed. The archaeologist and the historian have also much to offer one another, and a great deal of fascinating and valuable information can be extracted from documentary sources. Much can be learned harmlessly, an absorbing leisure interest developed and useful work done by the careful amateur.

5
How to discover deserted villages

Some three thousand deserted villages have already been discovered in England (see fig. 1). County lists of deserted sites are kept up to date by the Medieval Village Research Group. Anyone intent upon discovering new deserted villages should start at this source. However, our knowledge about each of these villages varies enormously and for many of them there is little evidence available apart from the fact they exist. Local museums or local archaeological agencies may also have gazetteers with fuller information.

The inquisitive fieldworker, however, should not be discouraged by the fact that so many villages have already been identified (fig. 17). There are undoubtedly many more to be located and of those sites which are already known we often have little background information.

Probably a comprehensive field survey will be the means of identifying vestiges of former settlement. This involves walking every field in a parish in order to identify areas of earthworks or in ploughed areas surface scatters of building stone, pottery, burnt clay and charcoal. Such concentrations of occupation debris are normally clearly visible for the first few years after an earthwork site has been ploughed.

Such field surveys should include the recording of ridge and furrow, either from ground observation or by extracting the information from aerial photographs. In some parts of England where ridge and furrow is very extensive it has been possible to locate former village sites by identifying the gaps in the ridge and furrow. A group of deserted villages in the area of Cestersover (Warwickshire) was found in this way (Baker and Harvey, 1973).

Secondary sources
A good starting point for local history and landscape discovery is the Victoria County History series. This is readily available in libraries, and some counties now run to several volumes, of which the more recent are generally the most useful. In most parts of

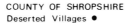

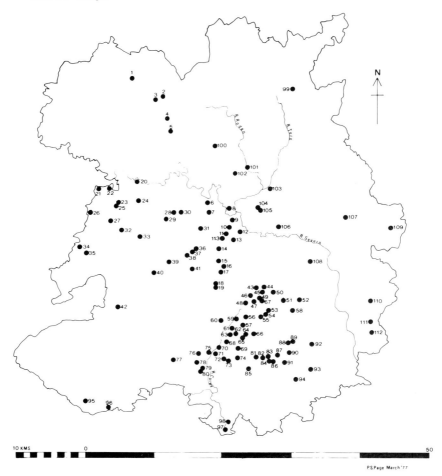

Fig. 17. The distribution of deserted villages in Shropshire (1979) – a county where it was originally believed that deserted villages were rare.

Plate 15. Winterbourne Farrington, Dorset. Irregular earthworks of a deserted village referred to in Thomas Hardy's *The Trumpet Major*, as is the gable end of a ruined church sitting in the middle of the photograph.

England there are local historical and archaeological societies, whose journals often include articles and reports on deserted villages. Nationally, the journals of the Societies for Medieval and Post-Medieval Archaeology cover material dating from Anglo-Saxon times onwards and the annual report of the Medieval Village Research Group provides news of current fieldwork. For more specifically topographical information, there is a series of volumes produced by the Royal Commission on Ancient and Historic Monuments. However, these are by no means comprehensive. There is a wide and varied range of secondary printed material and most counties now operate a local history collection where this information can be consulted.

Another major source of material has been established by county councils throughout England. Sites and monuments records (SMRs) are generally located either in planning departments or county museums and can usually be consulted by arrangement. Their purpose is partly to assist county councils in making planning decisions, but they also provide a basis for research. They usually

Plate 16. Barton Blount, Derbyshire. The clearly defined earthworks of a strung-out deserted village, showing a wide variety of earthwork forms. The village has been excavated (see fig. 10).

consist of a collection of numbered filing cards, indexed to Ordnance Survey 1:10,000 maps of the county and containing all the information known about archaeological sites of all kinds in the county. Some of them are in the process of being computerised.

Aerial photographs

An important element in most of these archives is the aerial photograph. Aerial photographs have been instrumental in the discovery of a large number of deserted medieval village sites; indeed many sites only exist on photograph as they have subsequently been destroyed. Sites are best viewed from the air, where the earthworks of a deserted village, which on the ground apparently form a meaningless muddle, fall into place, with a clear pattern of houses and streets (plate 15). Similarly, even on sites that have been ploughed it is often possible to identify scatters of stone, tile and other occupation debris, describing the pattern of former settlement. In some cases the sites will show as cropmarks, that is differential growth in a crop indicating some of the more deeply engraved features of the former settlement. The aerial photograph is particularly valuable in showing the site in its context, notably in its relationship to the former and existing field patterns, and in identifying trackways and other associated features. In some cases it is possible to marry a photograph with a ground survey to enhance the amount of information (plate 16 and fig. 10).

The fieldworker should be aware of the purpose for which the photograph was taken. Many vertical aerial photographs have been taken for planning and other purposes and record archaeological material incidentally. The best archaeological photographs are the vertical ones that have been taken by private individuals or by the Cambridge Committee for Aerial Photography or the National Monuments Record Aerial Photography Division. These two organisations have vast collections of archaeological aerial photographs and should be consulted by the serious field researcher.

Fieldwork

It is seldom possible to discover deserted villages by setting off at random into the countryside. Some preliminary detective work is necessary, and a good basis for this is the Ordnance Survey 1:50,000 map. A guide to former settlement patterns is provided by ancient parish churches. Isolated churches (apart from nonconformist chapels) will frequently indicate deserted village sites. They are not infallible clues, however, because often no church survives from a former settlement; in such cases a modern civil parish without a parish church can be equally indicative.

Apparently random junctions of footpaths and trackways in the middle of an uninhabited area sometimes represent an abandoned settlement. For example, the deserted village of Papley (Northamptonshire) was traced partly by the meeting of four footpaths and two bridlepaths in a remote part of Warrington parish. The patterns of boundaries can also provide useful clues. The shape of a parish boundary may be significant. Where the main settlement has been deserted parishes have often been amalgamated with others, so that an unusual shape for the area is produced. West Halton parish (Lincolnshire) is shaped like an L which has fallen on its back. One arm represents the ancient parish of West Halton; the other is that of the deserted village of Haythby.

Further indications are provided by larger-scale maps, such as the 1:25,000 and 1:10,000 Ordnance Survey series. These can be studied for land units and farm boundaries, features which helped to locate four deserted and shrunken villages in Charminster parish (Dorset). By comparison with other land units in the area it was possible to identify where settlements were likely to have been; a search on the ground then located them. Larger-scale maps also show field boundaries; if these present a different pattern in a small area of the map, being more irregular and enclosing smaller fields well away from surviving settlement, they can sometimes help to locate a deserted village. Field boundaries can also continue the lines of roads which now stop abruptly for no apparent reason, because the villages to which they once led have gone.

Ordnance Survey maps at 1:50,000 and larger scales often mark earthworks and moats which can represent villages and manor houses. The names of features on maps can help a great deal in the search for abandoned villages. An isolated farm may give its name to a whole parish, for example, suggesting the last vestiges of a once more important settlement. The names of the Oxfordshire deserted villages of Wretchwick and Whitehill are preserved in Middle Wretchwick Farm and Old Whitehill Farm, for example. Placename evidence comes into its own, however, when we turn from current to old maps.

Old maps

No systematic mapping of England was undertaken until the Ordnance Survey was established in the early nineteenth century. However, for some villages there are early estate plans, which normally incorporate valuable information (plate 17). One of 1583 for example shows a plan of the already deserted village of Fallowfield (Northumberland) and a Leicestershire plan dated 1586 shows 'where the town of Whatborough stood' (plate 18). Field names such as *Town Field*, *Town End* and *Township Field* are all indicative of a former village (as are corrupt forms of these names such as *Downship*). Empty plots of land at East Layton (County Durham) are marked as 'the scyte of the houses' on a plan of 1608. A *Millfield*, for example, is worth examining for traces of water channels or windmill mounds; *Blacklands* can refer to occupation debris which has discoloured the soil; similarly *Stonesfield*, away

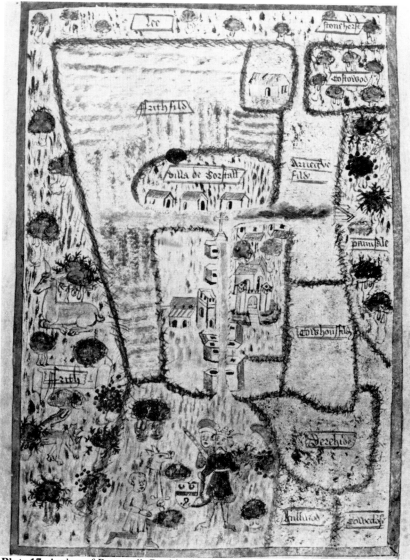

Plate 17. A plan of Boarstall, Buckinghamshire, dated 1444. It is one of the earliest surviving village plans and shows the church and moated site surrounded by houses and beyond that the village fields. The village has shrunk considerably since the map was drawn.

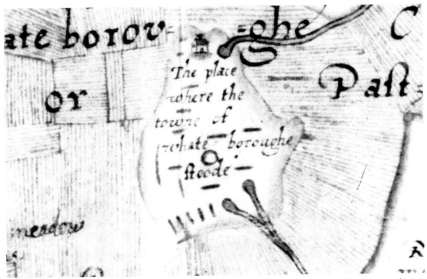

Plate 18. A plan of Whatborough, Leicestershire (1586), showing 'The place where the towne of Whateboroughe stood'. A single house sits on the village area which is surrounded by strips of the open-field system.

from existing settlement, provides a possible indication of a former community. The most comprehensive collection of field names is to be found on the mid nineteenth century tithe awards.

A useful link between old and current maps is provided by the mid nineteenth-century first edition of the Ordnance Survey. These early surveys are now important historical documents in their own right. The 1:10,560 (6 inch) sheets in particular show many details and landmarks which can be traced on earlier maps but which have since disappeared.

Primary sources

Primary sources of information are contemporary references to sites when they were still occupied. These include estate and manor court records and surveys made by government, church and manor to assess taxes, rents and rates. Not all of these are as inaccessible as might be thought, and many can be viewed in county archives. Some collections of medieval documents have been transcribed and printed by county or national societies.

After 1801 the population census returns can be used to identify parishes with few inhabitants, and those of 1851 and 1861 recorded people's birthplace and occupation. Caution is needed in the use of census material as a population of fifty in a parish could reflect the large number of servants and staff in a country house, where the village had long since disappeared. At Wharram Percy a population of thirty-five in 1841 became one hundred and seventy-one ten years later: but this sudden influx of people lasted only as long as was necessary to build a nearby railway tunnel. After this the 'bricklayers', 'stonemasons' and 'miners' of 1851 moved on.

Making a record

The other primary source of information is the site itself. Much can be learned if a careful record is made of a site, as the process of recording turns up many details which would otherwise be missed. A questionnaire has been produced by the MVRG to guide fieldworkers and is reproduced at the end of this book. Apart from attempting to discover the answers to the questions it contains, the researcher should try to make some sort of plan of the site, even if this is only a rough sketch.

The 1:10,000 (formerly 6 inch) Ordnance Survey maps can be used as a base on to which the overall extent of earthworks and ridge and furrow can be sketched, but for more detailed sketches a larger scale, such as 1:2,500, is useful. Although a sketch plan can never be compared to a measured survey, it can be of great value and requires relatively little skill. Apparently meaningless mounds take on recognisable form; and if a site is subsequently destroyed the sketch may have to serve as the only record of the site (fig. 18 and plate 19).

The method by which a sketch survey is produced is fairly simple. It is advisable to record several identifiable fixed points, such as the corner of a building or a boundary line, which can be subsequently related to points on the map. The site should be thoroughly explored by walking all round it, and the largest and most obvious features recorded first. The less obvious details can then be filled in. Distances should be expressed in relative terms, such as 'half-way along hedge', although, if the fieldworker has a consistent step, pacing out distances makes drawing simpler and considerably more accurate. Further accuracy can be achieved by using a prismatic compass to record the bearings of each part of an earthwork site. Heights of earthworks need to be estimated, unless an instrument survey is undertaken, and it is normal practice to regard the overall ground surface as flat for this purpose. Slopes and banks are generally shown by hachures (or tadpoles as they are called). If there is a level or theodolite available spot heights and contours can be

Plate 19. Theddingworth, Leicestershire. A shifted village (compare with fig. 18).

Fig. 18. (opposite) Theddingworth, Leicestershire. An earthwork plan of the shifted medieval village. Compare with plate 19.

earthworks

19TH C RAILWAY (DISUSED)

P POND
RIDGE AND FURROW

added. These should be tied into the national grid by locating the nearest benchmark (details available from the Ordnance Survey).

An alternative technique, more suited to smaller sites, involves the use of two or more 30 metre tapes and some garden canes or ranging poles. Here a straight base line is laid out across the middle of the site to be surveyed and measurements are taken off it at right angles. Although this should produce a fairly accurate survey, it is not generally clear where slopes begin and end, and for large areas a series of base lines will be needed with at least two people required to hold tapes and make notes. Scale plans can be made, depending on the detail required, at 1:2,500, 1:1,250 or even 1:500. For details of other and more accurate simple survey techniques and some useful equipment which can be made at home, the reader is referred to the manuals and surveying books available.

Whatever sketches and field notes are made, it is essential to label them fully and include as much information as possible. The record form for deserted villages, reproduced at the end of the book, provides a good basis for notes. The scale of any drawing should be shown. The direction of north should be indicated, even if approximately, and some means of relating the site to the surrounding topography is very important. The name of the recorder should always be included.

Once a site has been discovered and recorded, no matter how roughly, it should be made known to a local museum, archaeological society or county archaeologist. All work done adds to our total knowledge of deserted villages, and some exceptional sites may warrant preservation as historic monuments.

6
Where are the deserted villages?

The list of sites to visit given below is taken from a gazetteer published in 1971 by Beresford and Hurst in their book *Deserted Medieval Villages*. The MVRG is currently preparing an updated version, but until this is available it should be remembered that there have been considerable developments since the gazetteer was produced. Some sites have been found, and many more have been destroyed. Nearly all these sites are on private land, so permission from landowners and farmers should always be obtained before visiting them. The following deserted villages were thought in 1971 to have been visible remains of houses. The list is arranged by historical counties, i.e. before the boundary changes of 1974, and the national grid reference for each is given.

Cornwall: Garrow, SX 146780; Trewortha, SX 239750.

Devon: Badgworthy, SS 794436; Blackaton, SX 698783; Bolt Head, SX 715370; Challacombe, SX 694796; Cordonford, Little, SX 697745; Cripdon, SX 735810; Ford, SX 607615; Hayne, SX 748805; Hound Tor, SX 748796; Rowden North, SX 701765; Rowden South (Hutholes), SX 702758.

Dorset: Ringstead, SY 747815.

Durham: Embleton, NZ 420298; Garmondsway, NZ 346347; Hartburn, West, NZ 358143; Swainston, NZ 419294; Walworth, NZ 231191.

Gloucestershire: Norton, Lower, SP 138430; Upton, SP 152344.

Lincolnshire: Aunby, TF 022147; Gainsthorpe, SE 956011; Riseholme, SK 980753.

Northumberland: Middleton, South, NZ 053840; Ogle, NZ 137799; Welton, NZ 063674; Whelpington, West, NY 975838.

Nottinghamshire: Keighton, SK 542382.

Oxfordshire: Bainton, SP 578269; Broadstone, SP 353252; Walcot, SP 347198.

Rutland: Pickworth, SK 992138.

Warwickshire: Brookhampton, SP 319506.

Wiltshire: Gomeldon, SU 182356.

Yorkshire (East Riding): Argam, TA 112710; Cottam, SE 993648; Cowlam, SE 965655; Givendale, Little, SE 823530; Riplingham, SE 960320; Towthorpe in Londesborough, SE 867439; Wharram Percy, SE 858642.

7
Further reading

General books on deserted villages and the landscape

Allison, K. J. *Deserted Villages*. Macmillan, 1970.

Baker, A. R. H. and Harvey, J. B. (editors). *Man Made the Land*. David and Charles, 1973.

Beresford, M. W. *The Lost Villages of England*. Lutterworth, 1954.

Beresford, M. W. *History on the Ground*. Lutterworth, revised edition 1971.

Beresford, M. W. and Hurst, J. G. *Deserted Medieval Villages*. Lutterworth, 1971.

Beresford, M. W. and St Joseph, J. K. *Medieval England – An Aerial Survey*. Cambridge University Press, second edition 1979.

Hoskins, W. G. *The Making of the English Landscape*. Hodder and Stoughton, 1955.

Hoskins, W. G. *English Landscapes*. BBC, 1973.

Muir, R. *The Shell Guide to Reading the Landscape*. Michael Joseph, 1981.

Muir, R. *The English Village.* Thames and Hudson, 1980.
Platt, C. *Medieval England.* Routledge and Kegan Paul, 1978.
Roberts, B. K. *Rural Settlement in Britain.* Dawson Archon, 1979.
Rowley, R. T. *Villages in the Landscape.* Dent, 1978.
Sawyer, P. H. (editor). *Medieval Settlement.* Edward Arnold, 1976.
Taylor, C. *Village and Farmstead.* George Philip and Son, 1983.

There is also a series of county volumes by different authors on the making of the landscape, published by Hodder and Stoughton.

Fieldwork
Aston, M. and Rowley, R. T. *Landscape Archaeology.* David and Charles, 1974.
Coles, J. *Field Archaeology in Britain.* Methuen, 1972.
Hogg, A. H. A. *Surveying for Archaeologists and other Field Workers.* Croom Helm, 1980.
Hoskins, W. G. *Fieldwork in Local History.* Faber, 1967.
Taylor, C. C. *Fieldwork in Medieval Archaeology.* Batsford, 1974.
Wood, E. S. *Collins Field Guide to Archaeology in Britain.* Collins, revised edition 1979.

Case studies, excavation reports and detailed work
The excavation reports for many smaller sites, and much other useful material, can be found in the journals *Medieval Archaeology* and *Post-Medieval Archaeology* published by their respective societies. The *Transactions* of local archaeological and historical societies should also be consulted. The following excavation reports are of particular importance:

Beresford, G. *The Medieval Clay-Land Village: Excavations at Goltho and Barton Blount (1975).* Society for Medieval Archaeology Monograph 6.
Hurst, J. G. *Wharram: A Study of Settlement on the Yorkshire Wolds.* Society for Medieval Archaeology Monograph 8.
Rahtz, S. and Rowley, T. *Middleton Stoney: Excavation and Survey in a North Oxfordshire Parish.* Oxford University Department for External Studies, 1984.

A gazetteer of excavations at medieval house and village sites appears in Beresford and Hurst *Deserted Medieval Villages* (see above), pages 149-68.
See also the annual reports of the Medieval Village Research Group.

8
Sources of information

Local and regional

(1) Maintained by county councils:

County record offices. These contain considerable quantities of useful primary and secondary material including many tithe and enclosure maps. The archivists are usually extremely helpful with any enquiries.

County sites and monuments records (SMRs). These are housed either in the county planning department or county museum and can generally be consulted by arrangement.

(2) Museums. These often contain antiquity departments and some county museums maintain sites and monuments records (see above).

(3) Universities and colleges. Departments of archaeology, geography and history can often be helpful; and many useful courses, seminars and conferences are arranged by extra-mural departments.

National

The Public Record Office (PRO), Kew, London.

The British Museum, Bloomsbury, London.

The Bodleian Library, Oxford.

The Ashmolean Museum, Oxford.

The Medieval Village Research Group, c/o Fortress House, 23 Savile Row, London.

Cambridge University Department of Aerial Photography, Mond Building, Free School Lane, Cambridge.

The Society for Medieval Archaeology.

The Society for Landscape Studies.

The Society for Post-Medieval Archaeology.

The Council for British Archaeology, 112 Kennington Road, London SE11 6RE. The council publishes a monthly *Newsletter and Calendar of Excavations* – useful for those wishing to volunteer.

9
Glossary of terms

Assart: clearing or enclosure of waste or common land for agriculture in medieval times. Used as a verb or a noun.

Borough: a village or small town which has been granted a licence to hold markets and possesses other privileges.

Commonland: land in which the community had rights to graze animals, cut turf, collect fallen branches etc.

Crofts: enclosed paddocks behind peasant houses.

Furlong: a bundle of strips in the open field. The unit of crop rotation in open-field agriculture.

Glebe (land): land belonging to the church in a parish, set aside to support the priest.

Messuages: farmhouses and their associated barns and outbuildings.

Open-field agriculture: the most common form of medieval agriculture, in which land was held in the form of strips scattered through large open fields.

Plough team: the oxen which pulled medieval ploughs.

Ridge and furrow: the earthwork remains of open-field strips.

Township: small nucleated settlement, secondary to the parochial village, but sometimes containing a chapel.

Tofts: peasant houses with their yards or gardens.

Vill: a small nucleated medieval rural community.

10
Fieldwork questionnaire

Completed by...................................... Date...........

1. Name of county.
2. Name of site (if known).
3. Name of present parish.
4. National grid reference: (a) of site (NB: many of these on the MVRG lists at present relate to a modern farm while they should show the exact location of the deserted village); (b) of medieval church or chapel of village (if any).
5. Name and address of owner(s).
6. Name and address of tenant(s) farming the site.
7. Name and address of nearest inhabited house to the site, if not the same as (6).
8. Remarks and prospects for future preservation of site.

The site
9. At what height above sea level does the site lie, and how does this relate to the surrounding landscape?
10. On what kind of soil does the site lie and what is the geology? (You may find published geology maps helpful for the latter.)
11. If the village is on a slope, in which direction is it facing?
12. Is there a stream or spring nearby?
13. Is the site ill drained? (If not, could this be the result of recent field drainage?)
14. Is there a well on the site, and what material is it lined with?
15. What is the relation of the site to the church (if any)?

The earthworks
16. Are there any earthworks, and if so, over what area do they extend? (Very often they are to be found in several adjacent fields. Mark on the first plan the fields in which earthworks of the village can be seen.)
17. Is the site sloping, terraced or all on one level?
18. Do the earthworks form a recognisable pattern or are they indistinct and vague?
19. Are the lines of the *roads* visible? (These usually show as sunken ways.)
20. Can you pick out any distinct *house sites*? These are not always

seen as buried wall foundations but may be represented by raised platforms; and the positions of hearths may at times be indicated by patches of nettles.)

21. Are the house platforms contained within *property enclosures*? (These are either banks, buried stone walls or ditches, depending on the geology.)
22. How do these house sites and boundaries relate to the streets?
23. Is the village site defined by a boundary bank and ditch?
24. Are there any castle or moated sites or particularly extensive or prominent house sites in the village, and could they represent the site(s) of the *manor house(s)*?
25. How does (do) the site(s) of the castle or manor house(s) relate to the village?
26. Is there a village green? (This is usually a relatively level clear area in the village site, sometimes bounded by streets.)
27. Are there any ponds? (There may be a pond on the village green. They will probably have silted up too much today to contain water.)
28. Is there any evidence for post-medieval disturbance of the site, by quarrying or modern ponds, for example?
29. Are there any fishponds, millponds or mill leats nearby?

Ploughed sites
30. If the site is partly or wholly ploughed, how long has this been done and was the site levelled first by a bulldozer?
31. Are earthworks still visible in the ploughed field?
32. Are there any signs of soil marks in the ploughsoil representing ploughed-up buildings, yards and boundaries? Can you make a plan of them?
33. Are there any pieces of worked stone lying in the ploughsoil?
34. Can you collect pottery and other surface finds, bagging them by areas or fields? (If you have a 25-inch map record the field number. If pottery is collected by area, this should give a useful date range for the different parts of the site and make it possible to suggest expansion and contraction within the site, if you can collect enough.)
35. If you visit the site when it is under crop, are there any signs of cropmarks?

Ridge and furrow
36. Is there any ridge and furrow visible near the village? If so, how is it related to the village?
37. Is it straight or curved?

38. What is the width between the tops of the ridges?
39. How high are the tops of the ridges from the bottoms of the furrows?
40. If possible, try to include the outline of any ridge and furrow on your plans.

Plans
1. Extent and outlines of the site in the modern field system.
2. Detailed plans or sketches of earthworks, etc.

Standing buildings
41. List the standing buildings on or near the site and give if possible an approximate estimate of their date.
42. What are the building materials, (a) in the church, (b) in other buildings? Are they local?

The church or chapel
43. Does the church occupy the highest point on the site?
44. Is the church ruined? If so, how much of it still survives?
45. If it is intact, how often is it used?
46. What is the earliest architectural style, e.g. Norman?
47. What is the dominant style? Does this or the size of the church indicate a period of prosperity?
48. Is there evidence of a contraction of the size of the church?
49. To what style does the final period of alteration belong?
50. If the church is a modern building, does it contain any older features such as a font from an earlier church?
51. To what period do the interior ornaments and monuments belong?
52. What are the latest dates for the tombstones in the churchyard?
53. What shape is the churchyard and what is the churchyard boundary made of?

Other buildings of particular interest
54. Are any other buildings of particular interest or early date?

Documentation
55. Do you know of any documents mentioning the site?
56. Name and address of compiler.

Completed questionnaires should be sent to the Secretary, Medieval Village Research Group.

Index